NAVY

Simon Rose

MEDIA ENHANCED BOOKS
AV2 BY WEIGL
ADDED VALUE • AUDIO VISUAL

www.av2books.com

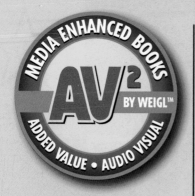

AV² provides enriched content that supplements and complements this bo
Weigl's AV² books strive to create inspired learning and engage young mir
in a total learning experience.

Your AV² Media Enhanced books come alive with...

Audio
Listen to sections of
the book read aloud.

Key Words
Study vocabulary, and
complete a matching
word activity.

Video
Watch informative
video clips.

Quizzes
Test your knowledge.

Go to **www.av2books.com**,
and enter this book's
unique code.

BOOK CODE

G 3 5 8 2 5 7

Embedded Weblinks
Gain additional information
for research.

Slide Show
View images and
captions, and prepare
a presentation.

AV² by Weigl brings you media
enhanced books that support
active learning.

Try This!
Complete activities and
hands-on experiments.

... and much, much mor

Published by AV² by Weigl
350 5ᵗʰ Avenue, 59ᵗʰ Floor
New York, NY 10118
Website: www.av2books.com   www.weigl.com

Library of Congress Cataloging-in-Publication Data
Rose, Simon, 1961- Navy / Simon Rose.
    p. cm. -- (U.S. Armed Forces)
Includes index.
Audience: Grades 4-6.
ISBN 978-1-61913-293-1 (hbk. : alk. paper) -- ISBN 978-1-61913-297-9 (pbk. : alk. paper)
1. United States. Navy--Juvenile literature. 2. United States. Navy--History--Juvenile literature. I. Title. VA55.R67 2013
 359.00973--dc23   2012021997

Printed in the United States of America in North Mankato, Minnesota
1 2 3 4 5 6 7 8 9 16 15 14 13 12

062012
WEP170512

Project Coordinator: Aaron Carr
Design: Mandy Christiansen

CONTENTS

WHAT IS THE NAVY?

The Navy is one of the main branches of the United States Armed Forces. The other branches are the Army, the Air Force, the Marine Corps, and the Coast Guard. The Navy is the main sea force of the United States military. This means it is mainly made up of forces that work on water. However, the Navy also uses planes and helicopters in its missions.

The Navy is part of the Department of Defense. This department is in charge of all branches of the armed forces except the Coast Guard. The secretary of defense is the head of this department. The president of the United States is commander-in-chief of the entire Armed Forces. The U.S. Navy is the largest navy in the world. It has more than 325,000 people on full-time active duty and about 100,000 personnel in the **Navy Reserve**.

★ The Navy is made up mainly of forces that work on water. However, Navy forces also may take part in combat missions on land and in the air.

STRUCTURE OF THE U.S. ARMED FORCES

Air Force

Army

Navy

Marine Corps

Coast Guard

Navy SEALs

Navy Divers

PROTECTING THE COUNTRY

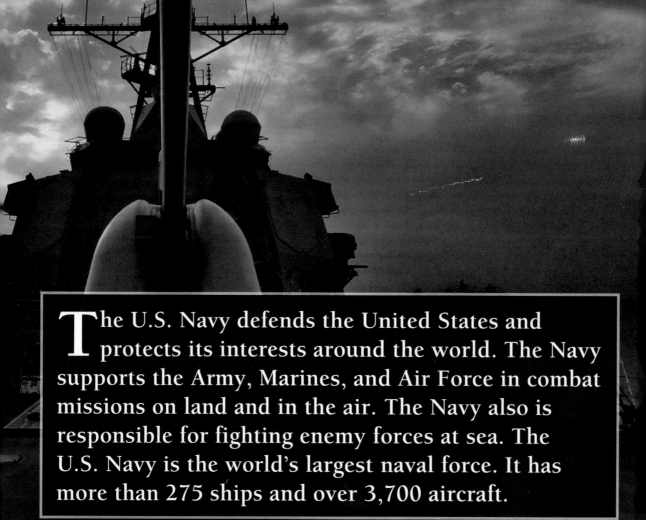

The U.S. Navy defends the United States and protects its interests around the world. The Navy supports the Army, Marines, and Air Force in combat missions on land and in the air. The Navy also is responsible for fighting enemy forces at sea. The U.S. Navy is the world's largest naval force. It has more than 275 ships and over 3,700 aircraft.

The U.S. Navy Reserve supports the Navy. The Reserve can provide personnel and equipment if necessary. Each state has its own Navy Reserve, but the federal government is in charge of Reservists. When needed, Reservists can be recruited into the regular Navy by the secretary of defense or the president of the United States.

On the Front Lines

In times of war, the Navy is in charge of the U.S. military's sea operations. It supports U.S. ground forces by bombarding areas held by the enemy from offshore. The Navy works closely with the Marine Corps in **amphibious** combat missions. The Marines travel on Navy ships and then attack the enemy on land. Navy SEALs are special forces involved in secret missions or small-sized attacks. Their work often prepares the way for larger attacks by the U.S. Army.

NAVY CORE VALUES

HONOR Be honest and truthful with others. Take responsibility for your actions, and always do what you say you will do.

COURAGE Make decisions that will best serve the Navy and the country. Your own needs are less important. Do what is right even in the most difficult situations. Be loyal to the United States.

COMMITMENT Obey Navy rules. Treat others with respect no matter what their rank, race, or religion. Be dedicated to improving your knowledge, skills, and character. Be excellent in the Navy work you have been trained to do.

HISTORY OF THE NAVY

The Continental Navy was created on October 13, 1775, at the start of the American Revolution. When the war ended, this force broke up, and its ships were sold. The U.S. Navy was officially created in 1794 by the Naval Act.

1783
★ Victory over Great Britain in the American Revolution

1815
★ Second Barbary War

1801 TO 1805
★ First Barbary War against pirates in Africa

1898
★ Spanish-American War

1775
★ The Continental Navy is formed

1812
★ The War of 1812 against Great Britain begins

1861 TO 1865
★ American Civil War

1776
★ The Declaration of Independence is signed

1794
★ The Naval Act officially creates the U.S. Navy

1846 TO 1848
★ Mexican-American War

1801

1898

The Navy has taken part in wars throughout the world. Over the years, its main work in combat has changed from battling enemy ships to supporting U.S. military missions on land.

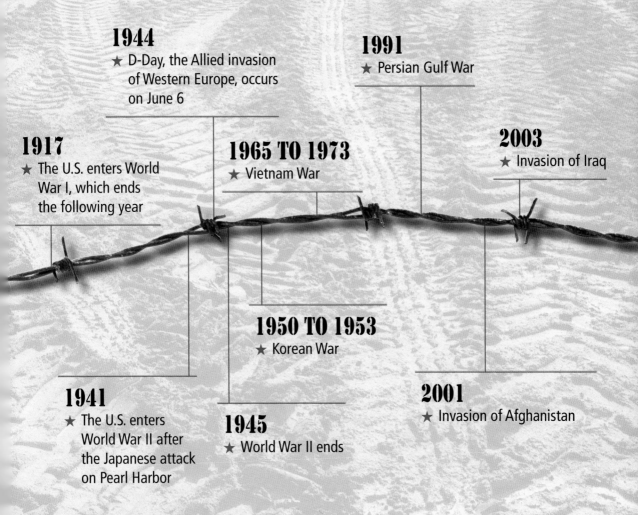

1944
★ D-Day, the Allied invasion of Western Europe, occurs on June 6

1991
★ Persian Gulf War

1917
★ The U.S. enters World War I, which ends the following year

1965 TO 1973
★ Vietnam War

2003
★ Invasion of Iraq

1950 TO 1953
★ Korean War

1941
★ The U.S. enters World War II after the Japanese attack on Pearl Harbor

1945
★ World War II ends

2001
★ Invasion of Afghanistan

1941

USN-702

2001

U.S. NAVY BASES AROUND THE WORLD

In addition to its bases in the United States, the Navy also operates bases in many different countries around the world. It also shares some bases with other branches of the U.S. military or with military forces of other countries.

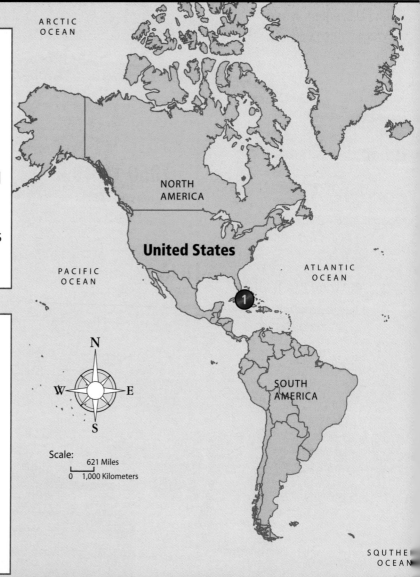

1

Guantanamo Bay
The U.S. Navy set up Guantanamo Bay Naval Base in southeastern Cuba as a fueling station in 1903. It is the oldest U.S. naval base located outside the United States. The base has contained a military prison since 2002. Many of the prisoners were captured in military operations in Iraq and Afghanistan, or in the fight against terrorism.

2

Spain
Naval Station Rota is a naval base that Spain shares with the United States. The base is home to the largest American military community in Spain. It houses U.S. Navy sailors, Marines, and their families, and also some U.S. Air Force and Army workers. The base is located near the Strait of Gibraltar, the gateway to the Mediterranean Sea.

ARCTIC OCEAN

NORTH AMERICA

United States

PACIFIC OCEAN

ATLANTIC OCEAN

N
W E
S

SOUTH AMERICA

Scale:
621 Miles
0   1,000 Kilometers

SOUTHE
OCEAN

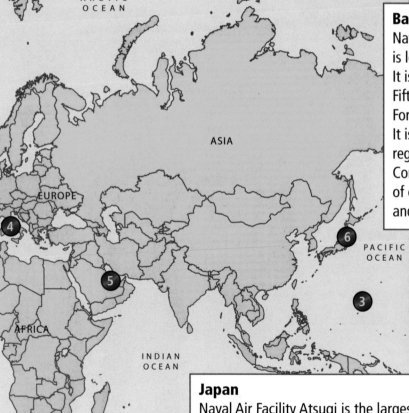

Guam
Joint Region Marianas is located on the island of Guam in the western Pacific Ocean. The base is shared with the U.S. Air Force. It is the headquarters for Commander Naval Forces Marianas and many other Navy units. These forces support the U.S. Pacific Fleet. This fleet is responsible all U.S. naval operations in the Pacific.

Italy
Naval Support Activity Naples is home to the U.S. Sixth Fleet. It is also the headquarters of U.S. Naval Forces Europe, which is responsible for U.S. Navy operations in Europe and North Africa. The base also provides emergency assistance if there are natural disasters, such as eruptions from the nearby volcano Mount Vesuvius or local earthquakes.

Bahrain
Naval Support Activity Bahrain is located in the Persian Gulf. It is home to the United States Fifth Fleet and U.S. Naval Forces Central Command. It is the main base in the region for Navy and Marine Corps activities in support of operations in Afghanistan and Iraq.

Japan
Naval Air Facility Atsugi is the largest U.S. Navy air base in the Pacific. It is the headquarters of Carrier Air Wing 5, which consists of eight squadrons of planes. These planes take off from the aircraft carrier USS *George Washington*.

ARCTIC OCEAN

ASIA

EUROPE

PACIFIC OCEAN

AFRICA

INDIAN OCEAN

NAVY UNIFORMS

The United States Navy has used many different uniforms throughout its history.

EARLY 1900s

Most Navy sailors in the late 1800s to early 1900s wore a blue uniform that was easy to work in. The loose jacket, called a jumper, had a 6.5-inch (16.5-centimeter) neck flap. A silk neckerchief was worn over the jumper. The trousers flared out at the bottom. The hats were flat and made of dark blue wool. In warm weather, a white cover could be placed over the hat to reflect the sun and keep the sailor cool. Some sailors also wore overcoats called monkey jackets. The back of the jacket narrowed to a point at the waist.

The officer's uniform was a dark blue coat that went below the knees. It had two rows of gold-colored buttons down the front. The trousers and cap were also dark blue.

WORLD WAR II

Sailors in World War II wore a blue wool pullover jumper with a neck flap. The flap had white lines around the edge. The cuffs of the jumper had one to three thin lines to indicate the sailor's rank. Sometimes, patches on the sleeve also indicated rank. Sailors wore a black silk neckerchief over the jumper.

Most Navy officers wore blue or white dress coats. In combat zones in the Pacific with warm climates, officers wore tan khaki pants and shirts when they worked. Khaki is a strong material made from cotton.

TODAY

The Navy Working Uniform features a camouflage pattern similar to uniforms worn by other branches of the military. However, the Navy uniform uses mostly blue and gray colors. These colors were chosen because they closely match the colors most often used on U.S. Navy ships.

Today, members of the U.S. Navy mainly wear the Navy Service Uniform. Men wear a tan, short-sleeved khaki shirt and black trousers. Women wear a tan khaki blouse and black trousers or a skirt. Both men and women wear a foldable cap with straight sides.

NAVY SHIPS AND WEAPONS

THE EARLY NAVY

When the U.S. Navy was officially founded in 1794, it had only six ships. All of them were frigates, wooden ships with three masts of sails. The USS *Constitution* was 204 feet (62 meters) long and had a crew of 450 men. The ship was armed with 44 guns, including 30 cannons. The cannons were mounted on **gun carriages** and could be moved around as needed. The *USS Constitution* is nicknamed "Old Ironsides." It can still be seen today in the Boston Navy Yard in Boston, Massachusetts.

THE CIVIL WAR

In the Civil War the Navy began to use a new type of ship that was protected by iron or steel armor and powered by steam. The ships were known as **ironclads**. Wooden ships had little chance of defeating them in battle. The USS *Monitor* was the best-known Navy ironclad. It was the first warship with an armored **gun turret** that could rotate completely around. Many ironclads were designed to be able to ram opponents to try and sink them. Ironclads were also used by the Confederate Navy.

The first U.S. Navy submarine to be used in combat was the 47-foot (14-m) long *Alligator*. It was launched in 1862 and had a crew of 12. The *Hunley*, a Confederate submarine, was 40 feet (12 m) long and had a crew of eight.

WORLD WAR II

The U.S. Navy's aircraft carriers played a major role in the defeat of Japan. Most aircraft carriers held more than 50 planes armed with bombs and torpedoes. The aircraft carrier USS *Enterprise* took part in more battles than any other U.S. ship during the war. It carried 90 aircraft and a crew of more than 2,200 men. It was 824 feet (251 m) long.

TODAY

The Navy's Nimitz-class **supercarriers** are the largest warships ever built. They are 1,092 feet (334 m) long. These ships are powered by nuclear energy. They can operate for 20 years without refueling. The Navy has 10 Nimitz-class supercarriers. They each can carry 90 aircraft including helicopters. They also have anti-aircraft weapons and a defense system against missiles.

The U.S. Navy's **ballistic submarines** carry and can launch Trident nuclear missiles. They are also known as Trident submarines. The Navy has 10 of these nuclear-powered submarines. Each can carry up to 24 Trident missiles.

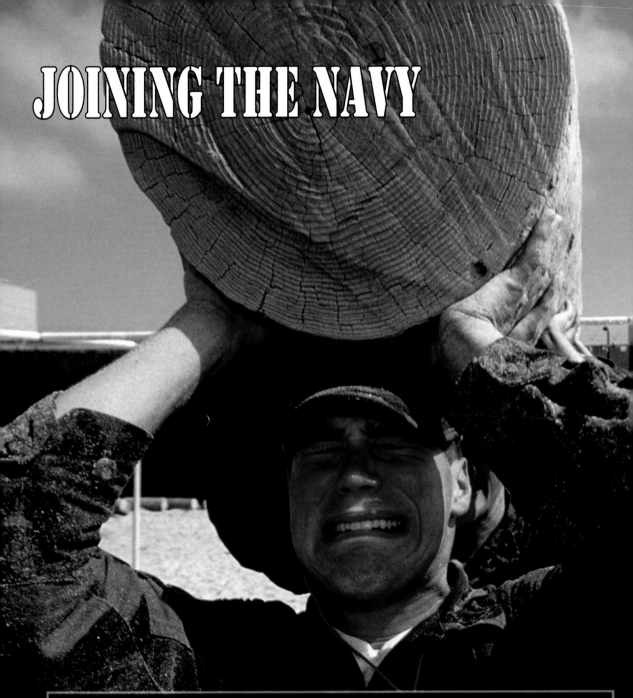

JOINING THE NAVY

Anyone wishing to join the Navy must be a U.S. citizen or permanent resident. They must be between 17 and 34 years of age, have a high school education, and be in good physical condition. Those wishing to enter a program to become an officer must be 19 to 35 years old. Some specific Navy positions may also have other requirements.

Applying to the Army

Step One: Talk to a recruiter

Step Two: Talk to family and friends

Step Three: Submit your application

Step Four: Visit the Military Entrance Processing Station (MEPS), where it is determined if you are qualified to join the Navy

OATH OF ENLISTMENT

❝ I do solemnly swear that I will support and defend the Constitution of the United States against all enemies, foreign and domestic; that I will bear true faith and allegiance to the same; and that I will obey the orders of the President of the United States and the orders of the officers appointed over me, according to regulations and the Uniform Code of Military Justice. So help me God. ❞

Boot Camp Basic Training for Navy recruits is sometimes called Boot Camp. The training takes place at the Great Lakes Naval Training Center near Chicago, Illinois. This training takes seven to nine weeks. It involves physical conditioning drills, marching, swimming, attending classes, and learning about weapons. Following

Basic Training, those who wish to become officers attend Officer Candidate School at Naval Station Newport in Rhode Island. This is a 12-week program that includes training in leadership and military strategy. Officer candidates also learn what is involved in commanding ships and submarines.

U.S. NAVY FACT

The first woman to join the Navy was Loretta Perfectus Walsh in 1917. She was the first woman to serve in the U.S. Armed Forces.

JOBS IN THE NAVY

Being in the Navy is not just about serving in combat. There are many types of careers in the Navy. There are jobs working with computers and technology, fixing ships and aircraft, and working in health care or as an engineer. There are also jobs in transportation, **intelligence** and combat support, business, communications, and more. The training and experience gained in the Navy can lead to successful careers in **civilian** life after military service is completed.

Aviation

Jobs in aviation include piloting some of the world's most advanced aircraft. People also may work on the ground to make sure aircraft take off and land safely. Other jobs in aviation involve maintaining aircraft weapons systems and communication and navigation equipment.

Emergency Services and Safety

Jobs in this area may involve putting out fires on ships and submarines or engaging in rescue missions. Working in law enforcement and security can mean providing safety for Navy personnel or investigating a crime committed on military property.

Health Care

Navy doctors and nurses take care of sick or wounded military personnel. They also may provide **humanitarian** health services for civilians in areas hit by earthquakes, floods, or other natural disasters. Careers include working as doctors, nurses, dentists, and physical therapists. Other jobs involve laboratory research or operating medical tools such as x-ray and ultrasound equipment.

NAVY COMMUNITY LIFE

In many ways, life in the Navy is much like civilian life. Members of the Navy work regular hours at a job, they spend time with their families, and they fill their free time with hobbies, sports, or any activity they choose. Some sailors live in barracks, but others live in houses either on or off the base.

Many Navy bases have all of the facilities of most towns or cities. This may include hospitals, schools, day-care centers, libraries, sports facilities, and shopping malls. The Navy provides a wide variety of programs to improve the quality of life for families living on Navy bases. These include counseling services, programs to improve on-base education and job opportunities for family members, and programs that help families cope having a parent working overseas.

★ Many Navy families must deal with the stress of having a parent work in a combat zone overseas.

WRITE YOUR STORY

If you apply to join the Navy, you will need to write an essay about yourself. This is also true when you apply to a college or for a job. Practice telling your story by completing this writing activity.

1 Brainstorming

Start by making notes about your interests. What are your hobbies? Do you like to read? Are you more interested in computers or power tools? Then, organize your ideas into an outline, with a clear beginning, middle, and end.

2 Writing the First Draft

A first draft does not have to be perfect. Try to get the story written. Then, read it to see if it makes sense. It will probably need revision. Even the most famous writers edit their work many times before it is completed.

3 Editing

Go through your story and remove anything that is repeated or not needed. Also, add any missing information that should be included. Be sure the text makes sense and is easy to read.

4 Proofreading

The proofreading is where you check spelling, grammar, and punctuation. During the proofread, you will often find mistakes that you missed during the editing stage. Always look for ways to make your writing the best it can be.

5 Submit Your Story

When your text is finished, it is time to submit your story, along with any other application materials. A good essay will increase your chances of being accepted, whether it be for a school, a job, or the Navy.

TEST YOUR KNOWLEDGE

1 When was the U.S. Navy officially founded?

2 How many aircraft does the U.S. Navy have?

3 At what age can people apply to join the Navy?

4 What are the largest warships ever built?

5 Where is Basic Training for Navy recruits held?

6 What is the nickname of the *USS Constitution*?

7 What base is home to U.S. Naval Forces Central Command?

8 What are the three core values of the U.S. Navy?

9 In what war did the U.S. Navy first use submarines in combat?

10 What is the oldest U.S. Navy base located outside the United States?

KEY WORDS

amphibious: operating both on land and on water

ballistic submarine: a submarine designed to launch missiles

civilian: a person who is not an active member of the armed forces

gun carriage: a structure on which a gun is mounted for firing

gun turret: a revolving platform with guns

humanitarian: efforts to save lives and prevent suffering

intelligence: information about the armed forces of another country

ironclad: a steam-propelled warship protected by a covering of iron or steel

Navy Reserve: part-time Navy workforce that can be called to full-time duty in an emergency

supercarrier: the largest type of aircraft carrier

INDEX

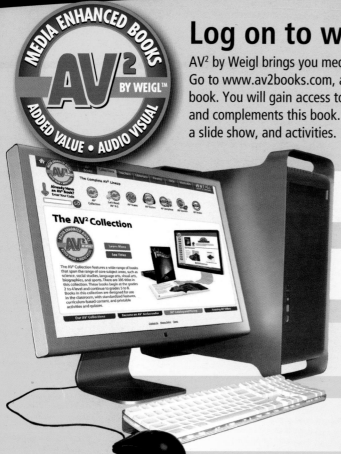

Log on to www.av2books.com

AV² by Weigl brings you media enhanced books that support active learning. Go to www.av2books.com, and enter the special code found on page 2 of this book. You will gain access to enriched and enhanced content that supplements and complements this book. Content includes video, audio, weblinks, quizzes, a slide show, and activities.

Audio
Listen to sections of the book read aloud.

Video
Watch informative video clips.

Embedded Weblinks
Gain additional information for research.

Try This!
Complete activities and hands-on experiments.

WHAT'S ONLINE?

Try This!	Embedded Weblinks	Video	EXTRA FEATURES
Try a timeline activity. Complete a mapping activity. Write an essay about yourself. Test your knowledge of the Navy.	Read about the importance of the Navy. Find out more information on the history of the uniform. Learn more about jobs in the Navy. Read more information about the Navy.	Watch a video about the Navy. Check out another video about the Navy.	**Audio** Listen to sections of the book read aloud. **Key Words** Study vocabulary, and complete a matching word activity. **Slide Show** View images and capti and prepare a presenta **Quizzes** Test your knowledge.

AV² was built to bridge the gap between print and digital. We encourage you to tell us what you like and what you want to see in the future.
Sign up to be an AV² Ambassador at www.av2books.com/ambassador.

6/13